Resisting Gravity
A Poetry Collection

Resisting Gravity
A Poetry Collection

Stan Crawford

LITERARY PRESS
LAMAR UNIVERSITY

ISBN: 978-1-942956-26-6
Library of Congress Number: 2016939779

Book Design: Theresa L. Ener

Lamar University Literary Press
Beaumont, Texas

Acknowledgments

I am most grateful for the help and inspiration of a number of teachers over the past decade, through Inprint courses and elsewhere, particularly Sarah Cortez, Mike Lieberman, Alan Ainsworth and Sasha West. I thank Sarah Cortez for her editing skills and help in organizing this collection, as well.

I am also grateful to numerous friends in various writing groups and associations for their suggestions and insights over the years, particularly Mike Alexander, Carolyn Florek, Varsha Shah, James Adams, Priscilla Frake, Jeannie Gambill, Carolyn Dahl, Rich Levy, Kristi Beer, Carol Munn, Lewis Garvin, Kathleen Cook, Margo Davis, Sandi Stromberg, Rebecca Spears and John Milkereit.

Thanks also to Bob and Carolyn Florek for launching the adventure of Mutabilis Press, to my family for their interest and encouragement, and to my wife Dawn for her unfailing support.

I am also grateful to the editors of the following journals and anthologies, in which some of these poems first appeared:

Borderlands: Texas Poetry Review
The Comstock Review
Five Inprint Poets (Mutabilis Press anthology)
Houston Poetry Fest Anthology
Houston Poetry Review
Illya's Honey
Improbable Worlds (Mutabilis Press anthology)
Poet Lore
Spiky Palm
The Texas Poetry Calender
TimeSlice (Mutabilis Press anthology)
The Weight of Addition (Mutabilis Press anthology)

For Allison and Julianna
and for Dawn, my first reader

CONTENTS

I.   Blind Spot

II.   Difficult Beauty

III. Out of the Essential Reservoir

IV. Light Everywhere

I. Blind Spot

Blind Spot

There was a time you drove
through summer's furnace, hermetically sealed,
listening to your own tune,
some golden oldie, and when you checked
the rear view mirror showed
no impediment

so you crossed the line
and someone's heart skipped, fusing
his hand to his horn a fraction
before the crash, but you never saw him,
never signaled
a change

and the time your son or daughter
said with a face clenched like a fist,
I will never forgive you for that, never...
but you didn't understand the reference,
your mind an empty plate
for this course

as well as the evening your love
gazed distractedly out the window and toward the sky
again and again, but when you looked out
there was nothing, just her reflection
in the windowpane, pale,
and darkness behind.

See how the mirror holds the world:
street lights glide in reverse,

cables swoop backward, heavy with words,
cars race toward places you've left
as trees spar silently in the wind.

You see everything you've come through
except your own part. You can drown
in water so clear
it reflects no light.

After Reading in San Francisco
About the Death of Ken Lay
and Consulting Orwell and Balzac

I scrutinize my morning face,
all folds and puffs.
Hair slack, gray-streaked,
random as straw.
A balcony of skin beneath each eye.

At fifty we have the face we deserve.
I too must be guilty of something.

Near Embarcadero a homeless man
with dreadlocks tangled as CIA plots
defies the signs that forbid feeding pigeons
and scatters his scraps of illicit bread.

Disheveled panhandlers and skateboard punks
hang on Haight Street and litter the park
with detritus of undertow
drenched in gold light.

Behind every great fortune, a crime.
A prison placed near the golden gate.
Sour inextricable from sweet
inside the chambers of our grapefruit hearts.

Icarus

O you gods who bewildered me
until I thought the air was a ferment of grapes,
until I thought the wind was a chorus
singing only to me.
Singing the one irresistible spell
that mirrors everything.

O you gods who took the wings my father made
and battered me with them on the rocks:
what was the point of your jealousy?

Surely you knew, just before my leap,
how my heart froze like a small thing
placed in the python's cage.

I never coveted the white ride
over waves that melted like snowflakes
falling into the sea.

You were the ones who made me drunk,
who made me forget my father's warning.

And men, if tempted to follow me,
remember how to find your way back
to land—our proper element. Know
how fatal a change of perspective can be.

In a Rent House

I remember clearly, most clearly,
how gravity grew stronger,

stripping down the summer leaves,
leaving our pecans and sweet gums

naked in the August heat.
Bewildered geese were struggling south,

breaking formation around chimneys,
swerving to avoid the occasional

dish antenna. Suspension bridges
sagged like untuned guitar strings.

All pianos were played *fortissimo*.
Sinkholes yawned, and when it rained,

raindrops hit the ground like small arms fire.
The moon loomed closer in the sky.

Our sleep was fretful, if we slept at all.
You parsed your words in shorter

and shorter sentences. Wasps crawled
along the floors from room to room.

We found their new nests hidden
in our cellar. Your eyes were green

as drowning islands. From the pivot
where I stood, you orbited away.

Aspens

There were months, years
even, when my anger
was a precious landscape
through which I was hiking,

a valley between young,
jagged mountains,
hills of scree and talus
and aspens. When I

am visited by old angers,
I remember the aspens—
so many standing
close together.

Their white bark
interrupted by
black scars
near the ground

where they were
scratched and mauled
by passing deer or bears
seeking food or medicine

and then above,
their slender trunks
sheathed in pale

green-silver leaves
agitating out of reach.

How I Saw It

That morning's light
held its shoes and tip-toed
past the windows.

Someone had spilled
gin and a little tonic
on the only map.

Three lemons on
the kitchen counter kept
a quiet vigil.

The raccoon who fled
up our pecan tree never
climbed back down.

Recycling trucks
came for everything
we would go through twice.

By 5 A.M. your eyes
went out like fireflies.
I loved you, off and on.

Cain's Complaint

Our deepest enemies are closest to us—
not threatening in the abstract ways
we may read about in the morning paper
or while surfing the internet,
but right beside us, smirking
when we go for coffee, or even at home,
humming the same wearisome tune,
always getting to the bathroom first.

Mrs. Smith surrendered her pistol
to the cops. Reportedly she aerated
her husband's spleen "...because
he wouldn't quit putting
the orange juice back in the refrigerator
in front of the goddamn milk."

Grit in an oyster won't always seed pearls.

What really chapped Cain,
even more than Abel's certainty he was most loved,
even more than his dung-dropping goats,
were the jokes.
Like when they were hunting
and Cain said, "We're not getting any ducks,
I wonder why,"
and Abel was all like,
"I don't know...
Let's throw the dog higher."

And then
when Cain's wind-chosen figs
and pomegranates tumid with juice
were rejected by God,
Who preferred lambs,
their necks slashed and bloody,
their white fleece vandalized,
and Cain saw Abel's goofy, bloody grin,
darkness filled every bowl and wineskin
in Cain's tent.

Cain suddenly thought
his rage was light
and he split Abel's skull
to let in the furious sun.

And God, in turn, banished Cain
to the land of Nod—a suburb
filled with ravens, dust devils and thorns.
Cain went, marked forever as one of God's own—
self-absorbed, radioactive with anger.

An integral part of the nuclear family.

Natural History

On my weekends we'd go back
to where things stayed in place:
the criss-cross bricks wedged tightly
over sprawling roots, white marble steps
worn down like soap, the neoclassic doorway
and inside, a funnel for donations
curved to keep coins up on edge,
spinning faster and faster through
an aperture into a void.

My girls were younger, more predictable.
They always went first
into the hall of Texas wildlife scenes
lined up like ice cubes in a tray—
a cougar posed, muscles tensed
to leap on a fearful mule deer
and rake apart his neck;
coyotes arranged in a canyon mouth
about to tear into eastern cottontails.

In time we stopped going back.
I moved away, then they did.
My mind still adds a last tableau:
a nursery scene lit by a lamp,
a sleeping child, a crib, and the woman
who was my wife leans over
to savor the baby's durable breath,
my hand frozen upon her shoulder
our eyes unmoving and unmoved
almost the last time

before we unbraced into our own purposes,
no longer useful to each other.

One Reason That People Hate Lawyers

It is like the time we visited the coast
of Italy, and were seduced by the apricot sky
and the lavish sighs of the blue-green sea
to go down the spiral stairs of the city,
past the shops selling beachwear and
lemoncello candy, and across the flagstones
along the water, until we reached the beach
slanting down to the waves—a sandy beach
that turned into thousands of smooth
black stones—and were induced to walk
into the softly curling water, deeper and
deeper, discovering on closer inspection
that the waves were colored a muddy brown,
rather than blue or green, and seemed
to be filled with ghosts dancing to the music
that only ghosts can hear. Suddenly,
it became clear that the ghosts were schools
of jellyfish, quite invisible from shore, but now
everywhere, trailing tendrils delivering lingering
stings like precedents or Sicilian curses,
and we fled the water, lurching and stumbling,
our tender feet pondering the hardness
of the unnaturally blind-black stones.

Home Again

My father shambles from room to room,
off-balance. Like a child's top, spinning
down. Mother's hips always hurt now.
She sleeps sitting up, curved like a
question mark, wearing her faded red robe.

A stain of rust where water has dried
from the slow leak under the washing
machine. Pictures of my brother John,
who died in 1998—Year One on all of
their calenders. Old spots on the carpet.

Six miles away, our childhood lake,
with the sloping banks from which model ships
could start their voyages. There once
were kibitzing ducks, honking, running away
when John chased them with sticks.

Our scale model of the *Queen Mary*
with holes in her hull is now capsized
behind crusted paint cans in the garage.
We used to fight for the right to launch
her. Not much to salvage now.

weak

The Minotaur on
New Year's Eve

In the next week
new ships will arrive and deliver

more victims to climb
the rocky hill

and enter his darkness
stinking of old blood.

The tips of his strong horns
—so sharp and sensitive—

his only way to understand.
Could it be possible

something might change?
His brain is a nest of tinder tonight,

waiting for a spark.
His matted forelock

is stiff with dried gore, and
tangled with doilies of gray

cobweb. His visitors will
smell of clean salt and wind.

Will he again run them through,
searching for the sea?

Force Majeure

I intend to meet
all markers and margin calls

but must insist
I am not responsible

if scheduled reinforcements
don't arrive on schedule,

if those on whom I depend
receive other offers they can't refuse,

if those who once gave me credit
now see me and turn to stone,

if the sky curdles and rains down
virulent toxic compounds,

if the powers that be
shuffle the oceans like decks of cards,

if angels of death arrive
with a shroud that fits me like a glove.

My word may be fragile,
    an unstable canoe,
suddenly sideways
    swept down the cataract.

II. Difficult Beauty

Houston in August

I read Zagajewski's poems about Paris
where the Bois de Boulogne dances greenly,
about spires in Lvov learning to fly
in the bracing Renaissance wind. What fate

decreed that he would teach thirteen years
in Houston? A bayou Calcutta, always
in motion, moving like a shark
that must swim to breathe, or a feverish

patient on simmering sheets. At two A.M.
groans from heavy trucks, perhaps starting
to collect the garbage, or maybe
delivering more. It is difficult to tell.

Our night skies with their radioactive hues,
gutters crumbling toward collapse, maddened
SUVs breaking out of the herd, looking
for something to stomp. Someone's angry child

pierced through lip, nose and brow,
silver hooks cutting her nasal cartilage.
Women on billboards along the interstate
promise a hot time. It's very hot

and what can we do? Perhaps consider
moments of difficult beauty: a dog's
red ruff flickering in the breeze
on its twisted carcass torqued by traffic,

a piano inadvertently jettisoned
on the road, smashed to wooden slaw.
Through torn clouds, the glimpse of
an unobscured star. Maybe two or three.

Struck

First, a section of sky unfurled
like a pirate flag, the clouds
dark as volcanic glass. Then
whitegold whipcrack. Air on fire.

Now reporters from all local
stations are calling his hospital.
How did it feel? He can't remember.
The wheel stopped. His number up.

At home a few days later,
several teeth loosen one by one,
give up, let go, fall out.
His gums are bleeding, and nostalgic.

His wife tells a friend he's never
been better in bed. Moving more
deliberately now, and a hint of new
electricity between the sheets.

At night he dreams he pulls up a long
net cast deeply into black water. Thunder
growls, like waves on a hidden reef.
If he opens a window, will it find him?

Refinery Row

Driving west from Corpus Christi Bay,
you soon see the ship channel towers—
those dingy silver refinery spires,
some flaring gas and flame.

Each day fathers and sons,
cousins and neighbors enter the gates,
walk the pipes, measure tanks,
don Neoprene for turnarounds
on the cat crackers, wearing masks
fed by pressure-demand oxygen
to monitor levels
of H_2S, acids and salts.

In 1999, as sirens screamed
and the earth trembled,
a black-yellow boil of caustic mist
leaped out and enveloped
David, Danny and Hector
inside the perimeter fence
as they ran for their lives.

In a sudden whirlwind of chemical ash
their world cracked apart,
though they all lived.

Daily, their wives trudged
into the burn unit
to see their untouchable,
unrecognizable husbands

stored behind sterilized glass.

Sailboats still danced on the bay
and the price of gas at the pump didn't change.

Storm View

Like curtains drawn by hidden hands,
a storm sweeps down the Delaware,
closing the bridge in howling white.
No way to Philadelphia tonight.
No compass star or moon to steer
a raggle of misplaced geese to land.
Sunken shadows in freezing air.

State troopers on the Jersey side
heave orange barrels over snow
to barricade the treacherous road.
Stranded myself, I watch their fight
through frosted diner windows near
a highway to the old Atlantic site

where Winslow Homer's lifeguard stole
a woman back out of the grinding
sea, along a pendulous lifeline.
Thrown from my iced-up window,
uncaught lines of yellow light.

nice

Dante in Texas

After months of drought in Midland
in the middle of a basin where the sea once tossed
(the sea now vanished,
like everything
becoming something else),
last night a spat of rain
fell against the plastic skylight in my kitchen,
making a sound so long unheard,
at first I thought it was caused
by some other element—
perhaps the crackle from an unseen fire.

All forms fluctuate through other forms.
Dante fled from Florence,
sentenced to burn alive,
burning then in exile with words.

Last night's rain
could have been a burning language,
summoning the denizens of Midland
through the sphere of fire to stand
under a night sky suddenly blessed by clouds returning,
tears of exile ended.
Summoning us outside to shed our clothes
and shuck our lumpish bodies,
veined and varicose from brisket,
beer and barbeque, chicken-fried steak,
more beer.
Though when I ran outside to hear
and feel the pattering music of the spheres,

the night was falling silent
and the streets were already dry.

American Gothic

In a sagging Victorian or prairie ranch house,
a family, or what remains of one, waits,
patient or impatient, mending or fracturing.
Simmering together as night falls.

Down the road comes a car with strangers,
travelers dreaming of wolves and gallows.
There is a river without any bottom,
its current faster than lightning or fire.

There is premonition. A birth mark
shaped like a burning flag. Bats or rats
in the bedclothes. Maybe irises bloom,
releasing their heavy smell, like a shovel

biting into a grave. Or maybe there is a city,
block after block of empty storefronts,
their windows blinded with plywood.
No one on the street tonight, except

down there on the corner, no streetlight,
no moon. Someone or something coming
this way fast, like a poisoned arrow.
It isn't God's fault. Don't blame God.

Dog Days

Just when we think we have escaped,
drought tightens its parching grip again.

Our own carbon footprints stalk us, while
outside our sweating bedroom window

mourning doves express soft laments
until heat stifles their cries. Rain braises

only the narrow coast, where fringes
of kudzu swarm, fecund as maniacs' dreams.

Trees near water explode in burnt green,
stop-action Hiroshimas. Shuddering,

my wife tells how a dreamed killer, faceless
as the heat, trapped her in a limousine

blacker than a hearse. From a brown
gunnysack, he produced rope, sharp knives,

duct tape, and one patent pump still warm
from the foot of a previous victim. My wife

couldn't breathe, couldn't scream. Then
the wail of approaching sirens saved her.

No. Not sirens. The hungry whine
of our skewbald, wall-eyed shih tzu

awakened her. The pet she saved from death in a Houston pound, returning the favor.

A Short History of Our Recovery

Having never lived with a weathervane,
I turn on television to learn how the sky
will change or darken, and if our recent
recovery is real. At this moment sunlight

turns our street into a golden cul-de-sac,
though down by the interstate, under the overpass,
the sun-burnished homeless beg for change,
parking their grocery carts in the shade.

Our cat stretches on the warm window sill.
Masked blue jays loop down the alley fence.
Nice weather, you say. *Let's take a drive.*
Yes, let's get past the strip centers lining the roads

like surgical incisions, past the insurance offices
and nail salons. The wooden boats of Saigon
have all beached here. Weather permitting,
let's find the real country before something new

arrives like a freight train in a wind tunnel,
before acres of homes shut their sleepy eyes
under plywood lids and return to dreaming.
We're doing okay, I say. At this moment,

our net worth doesn't fluctuate like a storm front.
The highways here aren't filled with refugees.
Although the headquarters of the secret police
in certain countries, some of which we call friends,

are said to be "fingernail factories," we are
blessed still to have our own fingernails intact
(white lunulae like slivers of new moon),
still helpful for use in clinging to something.

Weather Report in the Abyss

The compass needle is frozen north.
Snow, wet and heavy. An icepick year.

Trees glazed in ice
weep slowly, surprising
one last straggling bird
that tries to land,
grapples,
and finds no grip.
Beak dripping,
wings freezing,
no purchase
on black branches.
Trembling toward dawn.

The moon gleams—
an icicle periscope.

The trees recall traces
of lingering song
after birds have gone.

Kiss the earth and go numb.
Learn curses not uttered in ten thousand years.
Rub all body parts together.
Disturb, for a little while,
the hoarfrost that coats you
in white brittle fur.

Beauty in Exile
after Marianne Moore

It is inevitable, and yet
needs space to be. Imagine the magnet's
irritation with all it attracts—iron
filings, solicitous pins and paper clips.

The shepherdess hid in the forest.
As she bathed her white feet in a still pool,
enter Don Quixote, nag, squire, donkey
and half the village, offering her valentines.

We are not constrained enough to be
content with distant views of elegant
scales on the diamondback, the tiger's tail-
ored pinstripes, or the eagle's beak (as suited

for intimate encounters as a
can opener). "Compelled by experience,"
they flee. How white the nape beloved by
the guillotine. How swift the tipping point.

III. Out of the Essential Reservoir

Texas Ars Poetica

Though I am no Spindletop, no drill bit biting
deeply, deeply down into high pressure zones
far beneath the crust to summon stronger flows,

when returns are high enough even we stripper wells
are busy, drawing in shallow watery slicks and
skimming, ceaselessly skimming off molecules

of what is sensed in porous stones, in fracked and
    acidized
days, out of the essential reservoir. Kneeling, reaching
to claim what is left after depletion has been allowed—

undrained traces and hints, bits and phrases of hymns
hummed by prairie dogs in their burrows, glimpses
    of moon
between the goalposts. My pumpjack genuflects again.

Sandpipers

for Elizabeth Bishop

The strength of their attention
    makes them vivid,

waltzing on egg
    and mustard-colored grit

from broken shells, along
    the oscillating line

of luminous sand in foaming
    after-plunge.

Fuming waves, salvage hopes
    still enthrall them

after the gulls, skittish as corks,
    have flustered

out beyond the breakers, after
    lumpish retirees

have retreated to aqua, lime
    and coral timeshares

to watch the weather rage
    through tinted glass.

Though storm lights are lit,
    and wind whips down

the beach grass, rings the flag lines
                on their poles,

shoves around the chaise lounges
                by the empty pools,

the pipers do not leave the dance.
                Electron-quick,

thin legs whirring,
                they persist against

the melt of great green gulf,
                the roaring amethyst.

Invitation

Across one thousand miles, along the curve
where land is merging into wave,

hummingbirds are streaking south
before the sun can lose the shadow game

it's playing with the ashen moon. Leave
your curtains open; give me

distillates of flight and sugar. Though
my migration has been slow,

like the Red Queen I will furiously fly,
my throat choked with rubies, just to reach

the place where I have always been,
outside your window, savoring the scarlet.

Raise your sash—I have no other chance
to ignite this brief blue afternoon.

Lower East Side Kensho

Fourteen stories high, while a tape of Wallace
    Stevens played

The Idea of Order at Key West, I was peering
    west, over oaks

in the park below, watching night down-sluice
    the avenues,

shadows flood pedestrians, ...*water never
    formed to mind or*

*voice...heaving speech of air...*footpaths
    dimming under trees,

fountains disappearing, games abandoned, just
    the echo of

one basketball slapping the cement....Then over
    western buildings

...*emblazoned zones and fiery poles...*over cars
    and taxicabs

dodging up Avenue A, over the junkie nodding
    by the dog walk....

one last shot of sunlight launched into a bank
    of clouds

exploded them in radiance—backlit meringue
on pie.

A fading siren from a cop car headed north
thinned to a thread,

a stitch of bright sound in encroaching night. A
pair of high-top

gym shoes looped over a wire below the fire
escape became

a lotus floating in the dying light.

Cuzco, 1975

Before reading my journal kept on that trip,
I remembered the oils of the Virgin and Jesus
painted by Incan converts, how those canvases
darkened through centuries, turning brown
like the hands of the artists who painted them

except for the gold trim on haloes and gowns,
still bright from gold leaf mixed in the paint,
still glowing like sparks in the muddy scenes.
I remembered leaving the museum and the trek
up to Sacsahuaman, fort of black stones

held together by only its own weight.
No mortar, no iron. I remembered the storm
that roared from the west down the Andean rim,
the thunder drum rolls, the piercing rain,
the sudden slickness of the stone streets.

I remembered the Indian who called us in
from the deluge, and shared his Pisco
while we balanced ourselves on his wooden cot.
What I forgot: he had two daughters, not one,
and both were charmed by the German shepherd

owned by my friend, the engineer from Lima. I forgot
the potatoes his wife fried to serve with the Pisco.
I forgot his nephew, dressed all in black, who smiled
and smiled, and said nothing. I forgot the hutch
with two rabbits. My memory had sanded away

all but the general shape of his kindness
offered to strangers caught in a storm.
I forgot that his front teeth were capped with gold.
I forgot the clouds lifted as we departed,
how the Southern Cross sparked in the pitch-black sky.

Oracle

We were there when we were there,
leaning closer, apprehending
the moving fumes.
Before time came gnawing
and columns collapsed.

There was a woman,
then there was an old woman.
The hills vibrated
with cicadas singing
the taming power of modest ends.

Sometimes the hills were on fire;
this was one way
character was revealed.
Perseverance brought good fortune,
except when it didn't.

What was it
that we meant to do better?
The stars were naively beautiful.
Cold spring water poured
from the mouths of ancient stone animals.
The soul kept its own thoughts within the ruins.

Observed in Belize

You saw him first,
beside the sandy track
puddled with rain
white as café au lait—
a blue crab still as an exposed root,
one claw held high
the pincer torn,
his gray meat open to the wind.

Then I looked up at starlight
metastasized how many centuries ago
and given ancient names:
Invader of Shallows,
Breathing Bone, Cancer Nebulous.
Muzzy pricks of light
over the restless palm trees
shadowing your crab.

Let's close our eyes and dream
one eye acute enough
to see particular each instant lit
by stars ignited long light years ago,
kind enough to capture in its glance
a broken crab in shadow
by the tin-roofed shack
dispensing Chinese takeaway.

Moon Shot

Near Clear Lake,

an empty room
where adventures
were calibrated.

Success followed virtue.
(Yes, call it that.)

Now the gift shop sells
"Astronaut Ice Cream."

Command Central
computers
untended,
obsolete.
Their screens now
as blank
as the childhood
windows
through which
at night,
unable to sleep,
I gazed out
and up
at the moon
and stars

thinking

I cannot be
alone
in this.

The mind sews
rags of moon
into the sun's
white train.

Why I Do Not Apologize
for Gertrude Stein

There is nothing to apologize for. If I have given offense,
I have given a fence. There is no offence to a fence.
There is no sense in innocence.

We have no right to complain,
no rite to complain, no rite to complete.

If we never talk of this again,
we can never talk of us again.

Again, let us talk, talk again.

How could things have been otherwise?
If things were otherwise they would be other wise.
Otherwise, there would be other things.
Before I would apologize,
I should have to apologize for
there being nothing to apologize for.

Apology dies before
the words of apology die.

If I were sorry I would never do.
If I were sorry I would never do anything.
If I were sorry I would never do anything there,
for there is no there there.

Harvest Sestina

October already—a very long distance
from spring. Knives sharp for the harvest.
Autumnal processions and daughters to see
and I went, holding the wheel with one hand
along roads that twisted, broke and rose,
unfurling ahead like concrete sails

running before the wind. Nothing to assail
for awhile. Stars salted the cobalt distance.
My daughters, a/k/a Snow White and Rose
Red, chose their gowns for the harvest.
Melons, pumpkins, and late corn at hand.
This year's ad hoc royals to see.

My orbit taught new ways to see,
to tack into the wind, to sail
crosswise. The temperature stung my hands
too near the nest. A needful distance
away, roadside stands held the harvest.
A woman with a tumor red as a rose

near her eye stacked fruit in serried rows,
composing her still life. Her son could see
her designs as he counted cash from the harvest.
A king with his chest puffed out like a sail
started off the parade. Signs in the distance
said, "Vote for Jesus—His Kingdom at Hand."

Then a band, and the waving hands
of young women in formal green, white, rose.

A catfish moon low in the distance,
as boys with bad haircuts strained to see
their sisters pass. The tomato sun sailed
west, simmering over the harvest.

The road was fringed with cuts from the harvest,
uncollected by any restraining hand.
The tired king followed his sagging sail
of a belly to bed. The pale moon rose
over the swaying cane. I could see
waves like Evangeline's hair in the distance.

A rose in hand fuzzes with dust. My girls,
see them glide, whispering rumors of sails.
Not so long a distance to harvest time.

Woman Claims Cheeto Resembles Jesus
Hung on the Cross
—AOL webpage, August 14, 2008—

Silver flickering ghosts emanate from the TV. The Spirit
incarnates in fried cornmeal, onion powder and cheese,

monosodium glutamate, autolyzed yeast extract. Also
     reported
in tortillas, flapjacks and screen doors burned by the sun.

Hard times are when He drops in. Hard times. Diamond
     times.
The world is dew drying on the grass, a stream chasing
     itself,

but a band marches by, out of sight down a parallel
     street,
and we sense melody from a secret source—if not that
     reprise,

then some other, like bubbles breaking. The sea's
     immensity
churns and a million discarded pieces of plastic are
     saved,

to land on a beach in Alaska. Tougher than ivory, longer
than whalesong. All at the same time, on the same beach!

More than chaos will ride to our rescue,
          and Jesus comes into the corn once again.

The Wind That Blows the World Around

I.

I stood beside the slipway
under a Wedgwood sky

wincing to gaze across
the blue electric channel

waiting for the San Juan ferry
waiting for my eyes to bear

the palette of this world:
madronas curved like candied orange peels

larches reaching for the brightest air
stands of fir lending green reflections

to the burning water round
the islands breaching in the sound.

Later, landward dusk,
marzipan moon.

II.

Our time will come, the promised age,
a silver-golden hour. We ourselves will change;
we've been shape-shifters all the time.
No one knows when we'll dig an onion up

and gold will shine inside the roots.
We'll see the elephant, the seven cities
sweating gold like tears wept by the sun.
Thirty million buffalo: stampeding gold
coins on the hoof. White bones
to fertilize the earth. Dollars rain down
in the wind. Name the earth
and sell it. We will homestead
Avalon and Burbank, Pasadena, out to
the Golden Gate. No one can tell us
just how hard it is. No place to stop
before the edge, and why stop there,
we have the wings of our convictions,
we can leap like lemmings, keep your
filthy hands off my stash, now the wind
is up, the herd is running. Run!

If we eat, you can starve.
If we starve, you must starve also.

III.

The eagle spread its wings and launched
from a parching cottonwood
near a dusty basin.

Burning unconsumed,
its hunger sought some movement
underneath the fire-blue sky.

68

The eagle was not the tattooed gangbanger
cruising Huntington Park,
la culebra coiled on his back,

but it lived in his barbed stare
stuck to a woman who swiveled by,
her glance back at him a flickering votive
inside the cathedral of Saturday night.

The eagle was not the restless cowboy
drinking and driving north of Missoula
but it lived in the pulsing vibration
flowing through the steering wheel into his hands

as he aimed his truck toward the mountains
their faces hazy, but shining
like beautiful words in a language
no one can speak any more.

Bright as an evening spark,
the eagle rode the updraft over
gullies and shriveling channels,

over threads of thistle and tamarisk
stitched into salty veins feeding
the heart of a shrinking lake.

Under its wings, the wind was a thin
chorus of sighing, almost a song
to bring to the world. To bring the world back.

IV. Light Everywhere

Island Time

Beside the anchored ketch
we snorkel, dipping ourselves
in warm, lapping water
above bleached coral hills

above jumbled
jet-blue angelfish, yellow
black and pink
clownfish, parrotfish.

Everything under a high sun
strobing the water.
All offered just
to the two of us

as we paddle,
half-swimming, half-rocking
in turquoise swells
near the reef

where a broken sloop
lies on the bottom,
softening
in its green shroud.

A year from now,
we won't be together.
Too much ballast to combine,
in your opinion:

your ex-husband,
my ex-wife,
my debts, our squabbling and
disillusioned children.

On this golden day
it doesn't matter.
The storm that whipped
both land and sea,

that drowned the sloop beneath us,
after ripping its sails, breaking its mast,
pounding its crew with fists
of cold, black water

doesn't matter now.
All shipwreck moments
are superseded by
this clean blue sky,

by these
translucent fins
of white cloud
touching the horizon.

Your toenails
(meticulously polished)
flash red signals to me
when you dive

to touch
a velvet gliding ray.

We tread water,
weightless over ruin,

tickled by kelp party streamers.
With the placid
brown nurse sharks,
happiness noses in.

After Whales

Two days after Christmas
with the family, all together,
and exhausted by our own company,
we all decided to go on a daylight cruise
leaving the harbor in San Diego
to skim the deep water,
the kingdom of whales.
We boarded the charter
and as it chugged out
past the broken stone jetty
Pacific swells boosted the trawler's prow,
tilting us forward, then back,
like a game played by a teasing friend,
and we found ourselves smiling.
The kids bought tuna sandwiches
and threw the crusts
to cheeky gulls skittering
over the surface
of the blank water.

Four hours out.
Four hours back.
My eyes burned with wincing,
trying to extrapolate
whales from gliding dunes
of bright empty water.
Perhaps all remaining whales
now were plumbing
deeper and deeper depths,
trying to lower the volume

of acidic amplification,
the echoes from carbon-rich human life.

Still no living motion
around our trawler
chugging back toward the coast
except the ubiquitous gulls
swooping over
domed waves and
moving hills of water,
water coming toward us
like rolling silent sentences
surging without interruption.
Until,
thirty minutes from shore,
a school of silver bottle-nosed dolphins
surfaced on our starboard side,
then on our port side,
then starboard,
then port,
like olive-eyed jesters
tumbling before an abandoned throne.
We crowded the rails, shouting *There! There!*
They weren't at all afraid to approach,
tilting in the waves to observe us,
then chuckling to themselves.

Fortune Cookie

That years would be
    divided into periods
        of brown and blue—
Who knew? In my youth
    I analyzed Kant's *Groundwork*
        to a bitter residue.
Stoned on the abstruse, we
    Derrida detectives
        combed the libraries
For secret passages,
    coded analyses. Then,
        Enlightenment! Feng Shui!

Now just a bagua mirror
    hung above my door
        will deconstruct the world.
I put a few coins
    in a wooden box.
        Post hoc, ergo propter hoc—
Prosperity unfurls!

Moles keep making molehills
    but the Alps
        survive, complete.
Now my checks don't bounce—
    the wind is sweet—
        and my wife's feet are warm
            between the sheets.

Parable

I have read the ancient accounts
of how they arrive:
the sun is low on the western horizon,
the atmosphere is hazy
with a fine dust that refracts the light.
They are never recognized at first.
They are invited in, anyway.
They break the whip and leash of *mine*.

It is ordained that, before they leave,
the visitors must reveal themselves.
Sometimes their speech changes.
Sometimes their eyes become
bottomless.
Everything in the house
or tent may vibrate, and then
the lives of their hosts are forever changed.

Speaking about my own experience,
I get visits from neighbors, of course.
And from children selling cookies
or magazine subscriptions.
And salesmen asking me to change
my cable provider, or to buy lightbulbs.
I tolerate these interruptions
with all the good grace I can muster.

One night, very late,
there came a loud knocking
at my front door. Peering outside,

I saw only the ancient crack addict
who probably lives somewhere
on the other side of the highway
and pushes her rusting bicycle
through the streets where we live.
I told her to leave or I'd call the police.

But I haven't given up hope.
I wait like an old dog with cataracts and
arthritis,
whose master sailed away
ages ago.
I wait
for the day when he will return.
On that day
I will rise and offer
the welcome I've saved for him
once I recognize him.

Seven Years On
for Dawn

We were late to meet, even later to wed.
Friends placed on our cake
two small clay figures:
skeletons dressed as bride and groom.
We cut the cake and pledged our troth
ten nights before the Day of the Dead.

How many reasons we had for inertia.
Hard to forget
earlier dreams
snapped like discarded bones.
Now at night my breathing rumbles
like a tumbrel over cobblestones.
And you have shingles
though you are no roof.

But if we weren't together now,
who would train the honeysuckle
to twine along our fence, as you do?
Who would learn the names
of all the neighbors' cats?
When you're gone, our house is silent
and absurd.
You put red pimentos in my olive days.
When we dock in bed like two small ships,
I watch you sleep upon the nightly tide.
Your trust is the new cup I'm trying not to chip.

Gone to the Circus

for Dawn

As Lillian Leitzel enters the ring,
a clown-eyed parrot in a cage
on a porch a block away from us
hangs upside down and screeches, heckling
industrious martins and hip-hop jays.

I turn the page, and Lillian grips
the rings (her palms dry as ash)—
and she starts to turn like a human propeller.
No one below can look away
until the cymbals crash.

She trained her body to spin like this
by slipping her shoulder out of its socket,
which now she can do like doffing her hat
for she is *The Queen of the Roman Rings.*
Caution is dust in her pocket.

Then you wordlessly tease away
my book with a look that could singe
the afternoon clouds into caramels. We dis-
locate each other. The air crystallizes
and fills with calliope fringe

while an emerald skink is lounging
outside upon our porch rail,
consuming the old self it sloughed away
by chewing the shed skin with freakshow calm,
savoring the tail

as Lillian spins, and a woodpecker hen
pursues her mate up through a riddled tree
and into the sky (your light,
light blue eyes).
Days of resisted gravity.

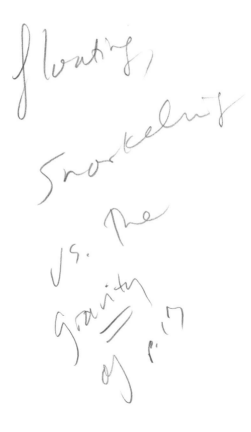

Paris in Mind

Recall a city through which a river winds,
and silver barges with crème brûlée soil
slipped under boulevards crossing the water.
Salons of chattering finches and wrens
mingle in flight near the Bois de Boulogne.

At sunset, chestnut-honey light embraces
mansard roofs, stone kings on horseback,
and the two mills still left in Montmartre.
Couples at cafes drinking under the sky—
the evening meditative as Satie. In a garret,

imagine me: Jean-Paul Belmondo insouciance,
outside the law. Imagine you: long hair tangled
on cotton sheets, inscrutable as the sphinx.
Love and lust, like dissolute cupids pillowed
together by Tiepolo in the Louvre, finishing

each other's sentences. A raven's fadeaway call
blows from the graves in Neuilly—a tincture
of death, small as Chaplin's moustache. Remember
Paris like a strange room entered at night,
yet somehow we don't stumble in the dark.

The Lemon Coast

Going where we choose to go, we moor
our rented launch beside the pebbled beach
and clamber up the craggy rocks above
the swaying blue-green water near
the cliffs, your shoulders ripening to rose
under ferocious sun, and so we find
a point beneath a slant of shade to balance on—
an equilibrium. A vantage post.

Put down the weight you carry, calls the breeze
that whistles in across the siren isles. And past
las sireneuses, near the harbor on Capris,
the shade of mad Tiberius is paddling
in a villa pool, its water laced with purple
flower petals, wings of circling gulls
reflected on its surface, and always sun
hung high and hot—a lemon blazing in a grove.

A bell peals once, and in this moment
we can turn, look north, and see
the mountain that the Virgin Mary opens
with a touch, to shut the Devil deep inside.
Her victory stocks the sea with schools
of white fish filled with tiny bones
that will be served to us at lunch today,
under red-striped awnings by the bay.

With our repast, melting *affogato* and
bone-white cups of coffee with a twist

of lemon peel. For this single day,
we do not want what does not yet exist.

*

Realization

This is almost the place, this beach of black stones where
      we stand
shifting our weight from side to side, hesitating before
the curvature over which we will return,
the unbroken surface of water
gesturing light
a sighing like promises branching off from the mother
      tongue.

There are, of course, alternations of light and dark, hue
      and cry
(hue of sweet, cry of salt)
and under a brazen ceiling of clouds
thousands of smooth black stones on the shore
and there is an intersection with soft curls of water where
armadas of jellyfish, flimsy and pale,
present as ghosts proceeding in time,
infect the waves.

There is a small boy holding a cone
of pistachio-green gelato softening in the heat,
until his ball of gelato
suddenly falls
into the waves. The green sweetness
unfurls in the salt in thin, dispersing tentacles
and the boy weeps,
understanding his loss. Understanding arrival.

But in order to approach the place itself,
we board a launch leaving at noon,

leaving behind bathers on the shore
(sorted beneath blue and white beach umbrellas)
(bearing dream offerings of smoke and olives)

The island shimmers in the heat.
The skin of the water white with it.
The island a black
intersection of stone and water
with the famous "Blue Grotto"
into which we drift,
through a hole half-submerged in the sea.
Darkness complete, except
for bent light
reflected up from white sand
stealing a hint of blue from the water
rimming the dark rock inside like a crown.

Across the galaxies
inside pockets of space
nestle black holes

but they are not black,
for light enters their borders.
Enters.
Not forced in,

but once in, held by gravity beyond our sight,
attracted by darkness as shadows attract snow.

Light everywhere in invisible pockets.
Light arriving inside the black stones.

We think we lose the light that ends for us.

It is not lost.

Mystery at 73 mph

It was Thanksgiving eve
on Highway 6, and sixty-
some odd head of cattle
were staring in unison
past our speeding car
and into the setting sun.

We were driving fast,
trying to reach Waco
for the scheduled feast,
just enough time to notice
the cows' synchronized staring
at a westerly stand of ash trees

and at the sun setting
behind those trees. (Though
were they ash trees? My ignorance
of nature is almost complete,
but I think they were.)
The point is that the "ash" trees

were between us (and the cows)
and the sun, which seared
their purple-red and yellow leaves
into all of our retinas like
heaven's freshest paints,
even at 73 mph—

and these colors leaping
in the rising wind

had mesmerized
the chewing herd. (Though
aren't cows color-blind?
Another natural fact

I vaguely seem to recall.)
But my point is that
the colors could ignite
a sense of the sublime
even in cows. Color-
blind cows. And

just then someone
in the back seat said,
*They're widening the
inner state.* (Or maybe
she said *interstate,*
but still—)

That was my epiphany
as we drove by the meadow
of the awestruck cows, and past
the Wayfarer Baptist Church
with its sign announcing Sunday's sermon:
Internet porn will ruin your life.

October Round

Wind comes from the north now
like a clever joke. The stars
repeat themselves and we don't mind.

Improbably blue days join hands
and stride by, fast and faster, past
the old escarpment, where live oaks

still glow green as brand-new
dollar bills. How long we've traveled
to arrive just here, as clean

as cats, and kinder. By midday
the gold is raised, the joke
is still on us and we don't mind.

This Poem

This poem is not the poem I intended to write:

The poem for women who weep young tears
of honey and almonds.

The poem for lovers when stars fall from the pockets
of plum-dark skies.

The poem that blends flavors of bitter and sweet into
dumplings as large as Rhode Island.

The poem that chases away shadows from our
marbled heroes, and blesses the metropolis wilting
like papier mâché in the rain.

The poem to heal our fractious republic,
to repeal the law of diminishing returns,
to reveal the secrets of the Rosicrucians,

the true value of pi,
the short solution to Fermat's last theorem,
the blue-green graves in Atlantis.

If I could write that poem, I would let you know.

Approach

Weave of white
pealed off above

foam blown
like old bone

a verging line
not tern or gull

but lit by
something winged

known in approach
wheeling shy

sly wind blossoming
a hand always

opening a door

Processional

Our feet will teach the road the way to go.
Beneath our names for things are other names
until we reach the place we do not know.

On a day like others we've been shown,
one thing is changed and nothing is the same.
Our feet will teach the road the way to go.

Just as a seam of shale will verge with sandstone,
memories will merge within our dreams
until we reach the place we do not know.

Above, the sky is vacant, and below
the blind and halt are gardening. Though lame,
our feet will teach the road the way to go.

Under winter trees, new seed is sown.
Our breathing blends together at the bloom
that grows inside the place we do not know.

With forms our empty hands recall, drawn
from harrowed air, a world is framed.
Our feet will teach the road the way to go
until we reach the place we do not know.

This is a book
that travels